The Last Prescription You Will Ever Need: Amnon and Tamar

by

Cyrené Wright, M.D.

THE LAST R̶x̶ YOU WILL EVER NEED
AMNON AND TAMAR

Cyrené Wright, MD

The Last Prescription You Will Ever Need:
Amnon and Tamar

Copyright 2020 © Cyrené Wright, MD

All rights reserved. This book or parts thereof may not be reproduced in any form, distributed, stored in a retrieval system, or transmitted in any form by any means - electronic, mechanical, photocopy, recording, or otherwise - without prior written permission of the copyright owner and/or publisher, except as provided by United States of America copyright law.

Published by
Scribe Publications, Inc.
609-961-1755
www.scribepublicationsinc.com

Cover design by Corey Scott.

DISLAIMER: The contents in this book is not intended or implied to be a substitute for professional medical advice, diagnosis, or treatment. Always seek the advice of God, your physician or other qualified health providers with any questions you may have regarding a medical or mental health condition. You are encouraged to confirm any information obtained from or through this book with other sources, and review all information regarding any medical condition or treatment with your physician. NEVER

DISREGARD PROFESSIONAL MEDICAL ADVICE OR DELAY SEEKING MEDICAL TREATMENT BECAUSE OF SOMETHING YOU HAVE READ ON OR ACCESSED THROUGH THIS BOOK.

Unless otherwise identified, scripture quotations are from the Holy Bible King James Version. Used by permission. All rights reserved.

Scripture quotations marked AMP are taken from the Amplified Bible, Copyright (c) 1954, 1958, 1962, 1964, 1965, 1987 by The Lockman Foundation. Used by permission. (www.Lockman.org).

Scripture quotations noted NLT are from the Holy Bible, New Living Translation. Copyright (c) 1996 and 2004. Used by permission of Tyndale House Publishers, Wheaton, Illinois. 60190. All rights reserved.

Scripture quotations noted MSG are from the The Message. Copyright © 1993, 1994, 1995, 1996, 2000, 2001, 2002. Used by permission of NavPress Publishing Group.

Scripture quotations noted VOICE are from The Voice (VOICE), The Voice Bible Copyright © 2012 Thomas Nelson, Inc. The Voice™ translation © 2012 Ecclesia Bible Society All rights reserved.

Any name referencing satan will not be given the respect of capitalization, even at the risk of improper sentence structure.

ISBN-13: 978-0-9967824-5-6

Library of Congress Control Number: 2020921207

Printed in the United States of America

Dedication

This book is dedicated to Cynthia Wright.

I am forever grateful for you.

Acknowledgements

First I would like to thank my Lord & Savior Jesus Christ for loving me, healing me, and protecting me through it all. You are truly my Physician! Your Word has been the prescription that healed me internally and transformed me completely.

Table of Contents

Foreword 12
Introduction 17
An Ounce of Prevention 21
Finish All This Medication 28
Expired Medication 38
Substitutions 42
Prohibited 42
Take As Directed 49
The Package Insert 59
Federal Law Prohibits... 64
Best If Used By: 101
Side Effects 109
Prayer of Salvation 123
Biography 124

Foreword

This book series is one that will challenge its reader with new thoughts and ideas on how to live and be whole. Using the Word of God as a the foundation for its instructions makes THE LAST PRESCRIPTION YOU WILL EVER NEED a timeless and insightful resouce for any individual, book club or Bible study.

Thank you so much for picking up this book, one of the first in the series entitled "The Last Prescription You'll Ever Need." If you are a reader familiar with our work or if you are new to these last prescription documents, then we welcome you to an adventure in healing and wholeness. It is in line with God's desire for us that we be made whole, transformed, and made new. Our prayer is this book will be significant in moving you through the powerful and effective journey to wholeness.

Introduction

It's time to divorce devastation! We've been stuck long enough! You may ask, "Stuck in what Doc?" We've been in a painfully perpetual period of being hurt and hurting others, distrust, despair, despondency, and depression from what has happened to us. We've tried prayer, writing letters, meditation, therapy, and medication, yet we seem to circle back to the same place of pain. Hurt has become your default setting. Cut the cord and end the cycle!

God's Word has given us the ultimate cure for life's ailments. The scriptures are the perfect prescriptions to bring healing, health and wholeness in every aspect of your life…. emotionally, mentally, physically, spiritually, financially, socially and any other -ly you can think.

As we journey together through this book, we will take an exploratory look at the story of Tamar and Amnon, an Old Testament account of love, loss and betrayal that will help to provide the template for a prescription that will unlock **Bible-based strategies on how to triumph in the face of tragedy.**

Let me add, this material is very personal for me because these are the actual foundational truths God used to create the scaffolding my life needed. I needed to shift my perspective, and trust when I say I REALLY. In retrospect, I see how this shifting in the way I think ultimately ended several cyclical personal struggles. When it was happening, however, I was merely following the leading of the Holy Spirit, unsure of where I would land. That is such good news, because willingness and obedience are "all any of us need" to extinguish the anguish that can hide in our personal lives. I am hopeful this work will ignite, refire, or cultivate in you a refusal to live one iota beneath the abundant life God has intended for each of us to live.

These works have become my personal anthologies of transformation because I realize many people can and do live hugely successful "external" lives, while their personal lives are riddled with repetitive relational failures with the same characters of different names. We can set up businesses and ride in the best cars but feel trapped in the pain of an abusive past. For me, at the time this prescription was written for me, I looked over my relational resume: social relationships, personal relationships, work relationships, it was all the same! They all started with the tingling excitement of "newness" and camaraderie and by the end, I was left feeling like someone had signed me up for betrayal, treachery, lies and deceit. I was at the end of my rope with it all. I would scrutinize my personal contributions to each relationship and always walked away with the same conclusion: everyone took advantage of my kindness and free-hearted love and concern for others. Ha! I thank God for the Word, it literally rescued me from living a life of inward deception. God's Word ended my inward cascade of bitter and broken stories of woe. It's a PRESCRIPTION!!

Suffice it to say, I am so thankful. Truth has taken me off the Ferris wheel of victimization and positioned me to love freely, live abundantly and hope endlessly. I hope you find that same liberty

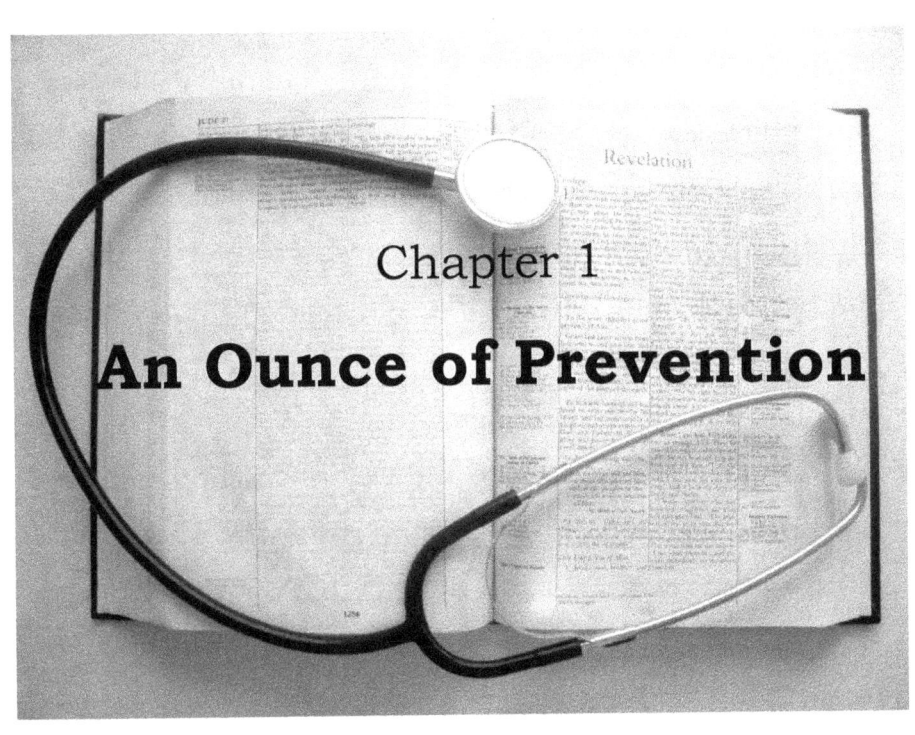

Chapter 1
An Ounce of Prevention

The wonderful thing about life and what fills life with joy is **the element of surprise**. This is, however, the same element that can bring sadness and agony... THE ELEMENT OF SURPRISE.

Think about it, when we have a neighbor mow our lawn or a stranger pay hundreds of dollars to buy our groceries, we are delighted by the element of surprise. Conversely, when a babysitter violates us as children or our spouse betrays us with a relative, those are the surprising and unexpected life events that bring trauma, disappointment, mistrust and a myriad of negative results for decades.

Both are a part of life and we, as Kingdom people, are not to live ill-equipped, not even for the unwanted, unexpected things. It can appear to be paradoxical to suggest that we can be prepared for an unexpected event, however, simply being aware of the potential for an event is part of an offensive approach to any dilemma. The best defense is a good offense. This last prescription was written as a guide for you to create your own offensive strategy.

To do this, we will look at 2nd Samuel 13. This chapter opens with the introduction of the characters and their relationship to David (Amnon and Tamar were half-siblings because they had different mothers). As we further learn, David was indirectly recruited to be a part of the narrative and part of the reason Tamar was present to be later violated by Amnon. Amnon knew David would grant his request to have Tamar serve him without questioning his motives. Unbeknownst to David, however, Amnon played on this relationship with his father to carry out an evil scheme

Right away, we find a key take away hidden in the scripture- a part of our prescription. People in leadership positions, like King David, may not be capable of preventing every evil from impacting our lives. They may not have the capacity, the courage, the insight, or the wherewithal to protect us. Most often, we presume parents, police officers, spouses and others will know how and when to protect us. When they do not, it can bring significant disappointment by both their lack of initial protective action and their subsequent reactions.

In this biblical account, we see that even though David was the ruler of his kingdom with authority in the army and positioned to govern thousands of citizens, he still did not realize his son was "up to no good." To his credit, when he found out about his daughter's violation, he was deeply grieved by his lack of awareness.

In a similar pattern, at some point in our lives, someone we trusted to love and protect us failed to do so. As uncomfortable as it is to acknowledge, this is a common place of disappointment. People with the best intentions and selfless hearts can still cause us huge disappointment. Devastating disappointment is a primary source of trauma. These traumatic impacts can be so far reaching and can be harder to recover from because relational trust is broken.

Keeping with our offensive strategy development, this is where we will mark the first part of our prescription: Forgiveness.

Forgiveness

In order to side-step perpetual "not readiness" and avoid as much surprising trauma as possible, we must decide to live prepared to forgive. Whether we have to forgive a disrespectful adolescent child to a rude stranger in the mall, anyone whose behavior falls below our baseline expectation requires us to be ready to forgive. This is especially true in close relationships like family, spouses, in-laws, and the like. These pivotal relationships demand a forgiveness strategy. Actually, relationships in the workplace do as well, any place where we are interacting closely with people. We must be ready to forgive.

Oftentimes, the people that have betrayed us can themselves be grieved by their lapse in responsibility to keep us protected; this reality makes forgiveness even more necessary.

Bear in mind, the necessity of the forgiveness strategy does not suggest it is a lightweight strategy. Forgiveness is a challenging principle to fully understand and even more difficult to execute, but we must live READY TO FORGIVE. What does that look like? We must position ourselves to be ready to access and release real forgiveness. When we allow it, forgiveness is a supernatural power resource. When we forgive, we create an inner place, an inward landscape that keeps us free to heal. The sooner we can forgive, the sooner we can be released. The key idea here is to keep our hearts and minds free to repair our own disappointment.

If we are deeply wounded, foregoing forgiveness has its allure. The key to sidestep the overwhelming temptation to be unforgiving is to never consider forgiveness as optional.

What are we saying here? Forgiveness cannot be overstated, but it is only one of the many strategies written in these prescriptions. Its importance and our other "prescriptive" directions can be found in Tamar's timeless biblical account, so let's look back at our main theme.

Like we have mentioned, the story opens with us meeting Amnon, the son of King David; he is desperate with "love" for Tamar, his half-sister.

As the story continues, we find that an evil plan was devised by Amnon and his cousin Jonadab to say Amnon was sick so that Tamar would, upon his request to the king, come to his house to care for him and prepare a meal. Their father, King David, agreed to his request and sent Tamar to Amnon's home to fulfill his wishes. In reality, he had faked being sick so that he could get this alone time with Tamar. It is not unveiled until the middle of the story that his full plan was not only to have her come his home but to also have sex with her.

It is important to note that during biblical times, if a virgin had sex outside of marriage, she became an outcast. Now imagine the additional shame of her virginity being taken by her brother. For Tamar to have been violated by her brother carried personal trauma as well as a stigma of disgrace to the territory, her family, and her God. This is why he needed such an elaborate scheme to lure her to his house to carry out this awful plan.

The scripture shows us he did ultimately rape her and as soon as he was done raping her, he turned on her and the scripture says he "*hated*" her. Once he had satisfied his overwhelming "*love*" – **his words for her** – through **RAPE**, he had his servants put her out of his house.

What Amnon had initially felt as love for Tamar quickly turned to deep disdain and hatred. The Bible account says his hatred was greater than the love he had. She was kicked out of the house and the door locked behind her. YES, HE LITERALLY KICKED HER OUT!! This was not only tragic, but it was also so unexpected.

As difficult as this time is for Tamar, this is where we will dig more into building our next offensive strategy.

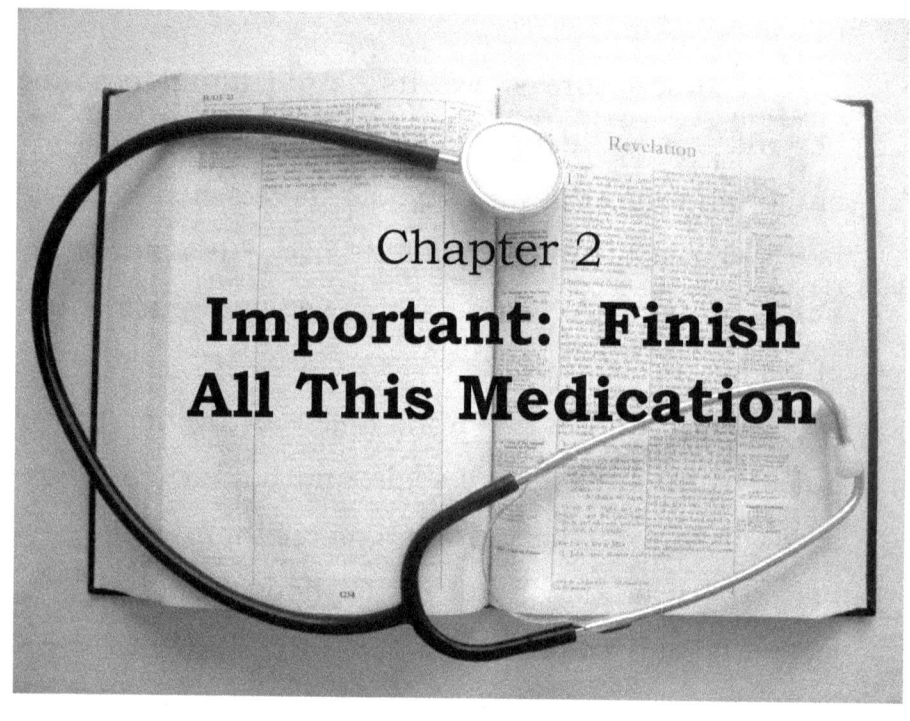

Chapter 2
Important: Finish All This Medication

Finish all of this medication

Before we dive in deeper, let's do some housekeeping. The fact of the matter is this: wisdom can be learned from the pain of personal experience or by observing others. I am writing this prescription to share the wisdom I gained from Tamar's experience, since we are not having this exact same experience as she did, my goal is to unfold that same wisdom for you.

As I make observations and consider hypotheticals related to this account, I will also point out areas where my personal lessons were learned. There is only one rule as we investigate, we will not seek to blame!

My parenthetical disclaimer about the idea of blaming: in any circumstance in your life or my own it is not wise to "look back" at someone's reaction or your own and find blame. The reality is, when we look in what is called "hindsight," we can see things very clearly. The context of the situation is inverted because the stressors are gone. In retrospect, we can always devise reactions that may not have been so clear to us or the parties involved IN THAT MOMENT. To that end, we only look back to investigate and learn, never blame.

That being said, let us forge into our look back and consider what we knew about Tamar before all of this occurred. If we think of who Tamar was before all of this, Tamar was a princess, the daughter of the king. There was no mention of her before or after this account. It can be said that her life's circumstances were perhaps uneventful. We can speculate the following: she was likely expecting to be married, she could continue her life as royalty, she could train other royal woman to be responsible for social events or perhaps participate in regional events. Whatever her plans were, nothing about her life was scripturally notable until she became a part of Amnon's plan.

Amnon's plan, even though it was contrived and self-serving, was not meant to bring devastation into her life. His only plan was to indulge his overwhelming desire for her. Unfortunately, the narrow lens of selfishness leaves its players blind to how hurtful their actions can be. The more selfish someone's agenda, the less likely they have considered how it will impact others.

As the story goes, she was, in fact, used by him. She was forced. She was acted upon in a violent way. Manipulated. Her innocence preyed upon. She was totally taken advantage of and our first offensive point, is still the strongest. We must live knowing that even when we are face-to-face with a traumatic event, we are always empowered to apply strategy #1: forgiveness.

Now it is also true, when we are assaulted or betrayed or violated, there is more chance for trauma, and therefore more barriers to get to the bottom of the medicine bottle. Yes, forgiveness opens "the bottle;" this is why, in our earlier discussion, we defined forgiveness as the superpower that liberates us. What we are adding to this strategy now with the "take all your medicine approach" is the additional push to extract the wisdom and maturity from the experience, no matter what!!

Just like the other parts of our strategy, this part of the strategy is offensive: self–directed and pre-planned. We have to decide how we will move forward BEFORE anything actually happens. What helped me side-step feeling mistreated and preyed upon was this: I could have preset rules for what I would accept in relationships and use them to respond. Even more, I could also predetermine my recovery strategy! Before this realization, I was always ONLY reacting...on and in constant defense mode. Yes, I know, easier said than done and yes, I am writing this retrospectively, but when it was happening in real time, I clearly had no preplanned strategy for how to respond if I encountered anything unexpected. I had no plan. No emotional plan, no recovery plan, no substantive view of who I was as a "recoverer." I would actually quote recovery scriptures but had not pre-planned a recovery. Here is one from the book of Philippians: "I can do all things through Christ who strengthens me." That is a "one size fits all" recovery scripture. My situations qualified as "all things," which meant the recovery plan in the Scripture was available for me to follow, but I did not apply this strategy to my situation. My thoughts did not remain in Him. I did not seek guidance through Him. I did not rely on His strength and gain His strength to do it. I had quoted it, but I had not used my resources to preplan. I was so off centered. Even when Holy Spirit began to unlock some of these very principles in front of me, I had to admit I was not exactly ready. I would not even open "my mouth to take the medicine," so I definitely was not ready to finish the bottle.

    Listen, one thing that I am hopeful will leap from the pages of this book is compassion. I too have been where you are and truth be told, I am a work in progress and am striving daily to stay steadfast in my healing and in uncompromising truth. This journey has not been easy by any means but when I finally stopped fight and decided to REALLY take ALL of my prescriptions, I began to reap the benefits of a healed heart, a healthy mindset and a whole spirit.

Healing is ours to possess, but it is not without effort. I remember making the transition from finally knowing what to do and doing it. They simply are not the same things, especially when they are occurring at nearly the same time. Just like the dual action required for a childproof twist caps, recovery of this sort is not for those who cannot push and twist. I had to learn and do simultaneously so will some of you! So, I say to you like I did to myself...no matter how devastated, how betrayed, or how violated, how unjust, we have to take all of our medicine.

Let me add this last crucial step; the place where knowing what to do and doing the thing we know to do is called commitment. I have created a euphemism "take all your medicine" because the Kingdom requires commitment. In order to recover and negotiate the unexpected events of life, we must commit to the process. Commit to the growth. Commit to it with tears. Commit to it while being misunderstood. Face the agony and the loneliness. Commit to be courageous for yourself. Commitment to ask the hard questions. Commit to allow pain to hurt because you're transforming that pain into power.

I was finally in the place of completing circles instead of walking in circles. When I looked back at the commitment and how much there was to accomplish, I could see how the pieces fit together.

This level of commitment can only happen if we do what? If we forgive. It is no coincidence we keep circling back to forgiveness. There is an intrinsic connection between "taking all the medicine" (extracting the wisdom and being open to the maturity of an experience) and forgiveness.

We have parenthetically described forgiveness a couple of different ways, one of which is a superpower that opens the "bottle". That is because I have found that forgiveness creates a scaffolding in our hearts that gives us the capacity to make the commitment. Commit to all of the process that lies ahead.

Commitment partners with clarity, and together they plow us through the hard places with a bullseye target on the wisdom we need to mature and flourish. Listen to me when I tell you, at the point we gain clarity in the aftermath of trauma, we are winning! These "unexpecteds" involve high unfiltered emotional reactions and high emotional places are rarely places of clarity. WE may not arrive here instantaneously, but the sooner we can be clear, the more likely we can avoid trauma's residue turning our life in directions it was never intended to go. Even though this "finish the bottle" principle can take time, when we challenge ourselves in this way, we are well on our way to maturity and healing.

I am going to add this important doctrinal concept now. It is not biblically supported and doctrinally true to suggest, infer, or imply God must torture us with disappointment and pain to bring us to any transformative place. That is not true or truth! As Kingdom Believers, we must always approach the Word of God from the basis of God's self-defined character of love. A simple and profound truth fits well here: life's experiences are carried out by people. God's desires for us are good. This will assist us in refusing to commit to being abused or redefining the intent of some evil incident as an agent of God's attempt to bring change. What is true? As we encounter unexpected pain and tragedy in the experience of life, with a Kingdom based prescription, we can clearly identify the elements of wisdom intrinsically held inside of traumatic events and make the right wise decisions to heal.

It is God's grace and His ability to access that supernatural grace that allows this process. In the aftermath of any unexpected occurrence, we need to restructure our understanding, possibly recreate internal landscapes and capitalize on our ability to switch losses to gains.

All this being said, we know that many have not forgiven or been forgiven. The misfortune to all involved are the missed opportunities to extract the highest wisdom hidden inside those experiences.

With this in front of us, it is easier to see how Tamar's outcome and, more importantly some of our own outcomes, can be changed by applying these ideas. It is often the case; we can see where others are repeating negative cycles more easily than we can see our own. In the proactive pattern of this prescription, let's create this declaration: **no matter how painful, I**

will not waste any opportunity in my life to heal grow and gain wisdom.

So, let us see where we are. We live ready to forgive and have tracked that forgiveness through to an uncluttered path of wisdom and healing.

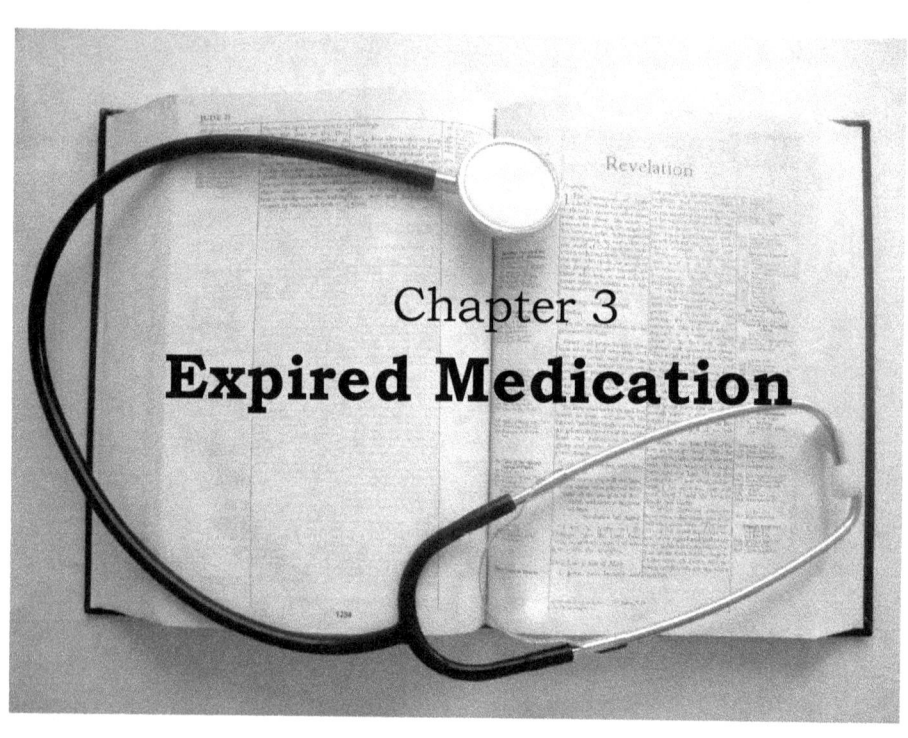

Chapter 3
Expired Medication

Last Rx You'll Ever Need

What are some of the possibilities that hindered Tamar from making transitioning from trauma to wisdom and healing? Most likely, the same things that complicate this transition for us. Wasting the wisdom of a traumatic experience never feels like waste at the time it is occurring. At the time, the forfeiture of extracting wisdom and growing when we have been wronged hides in our "right to be angry". Let's consider that for a moment. When we have been violated, let's say surprised by the unfavorable surprises of life, we likely have the right to be angry. In my opinion it is so foolish to suggest, we must skip over the very normal feeling of anger when we have faced one of these situations

The danger of expressing anger when someone makes us angry only happens when we use that anger as our only resource to soothe our pain. This is how this looked in my life, whenever someone mentioned the situation or a person, in a matter of seconds, my mind would arrive right back at the episode with all the players in their respective places, saying all of their respective lines, merely to bring me back to the conclusion, I had been wronged.

Anger became the medicine I chose, not the prescription I needed. I chose it as a medicine because it provided temporary relief. I was content to resentence the other party in the prison of my mental rehearsals, until I realized the only way to sustain that temporary relief was with bitterness.

See that is just it. If perpetual "angry validations" were not seeds of bitterness, we would have a very different conversation. That is exactly what they are! We must deal with bitterness just like we deal with expired medication. Throw it out immediately! Throw out advice from bitter people! Throw out ALL the bitter conversations you have heard over the years! Throw out all the social media influencers that are bitter! Throw out all the podcasts hosted by bitter people! Throw out the self-deprecating rewards of bitterness! Throw it ALL out!! Just like expired medication, it is ineffective, it is potentially toxic, and the side effect profile can include death.

If you are like me you are thinking, "easy for her to say, excruciating for me to do." Trust me when I tell you, when this prescription was written for me, I thought surely, I had been given the wrong "bag" at the pharmacy window of Heaven. It is comical now but not exactly funny how I had deputized myself as my own emotional vindicator and was pinning a badge of bitterness on my emotional wall daily. Yes, I was forfeiting the wisdom and I had erroneously decided wisdom was not a factor. Actually, I was not only wasting wisdom, I was also wasting time.

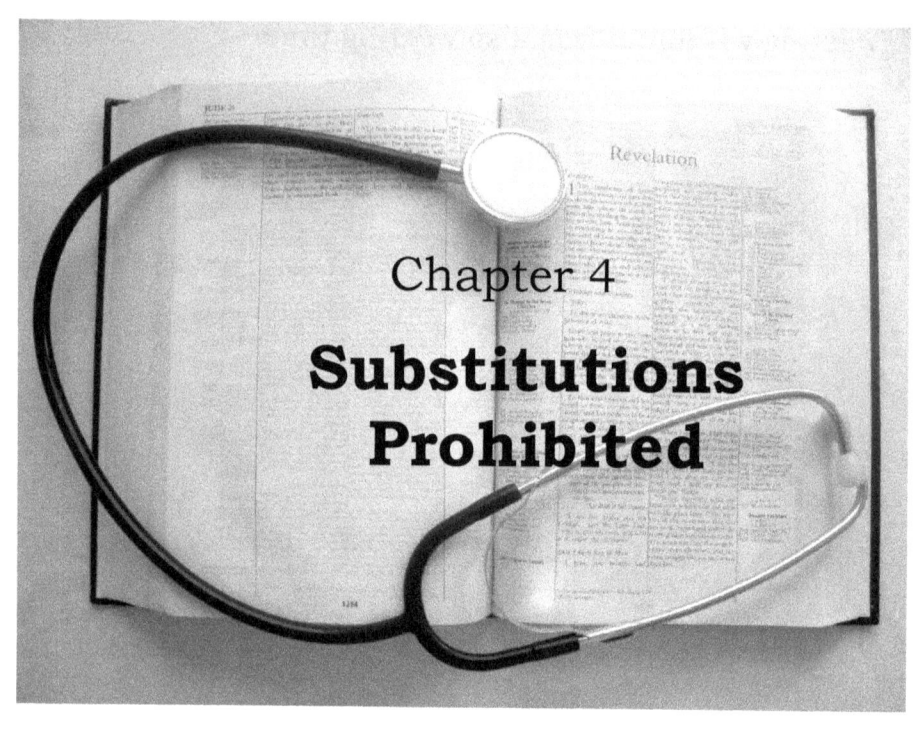

Chapter 4
Substitutions Prohibited

We are in the home stretch now. We are ACTIVELY building our prescription as a pre-planned offensive approach to those situations in life that are unwanted and unexpected. Tamar (our scriptural point of reference) is where we are taking our look back to create said approach.

As we forge ahead, we are just a few sentences away from grabbing a clear glass of water and paying close attention to our instructions. We are not going to use transient, soothing emotions that have bitterness as a price tag; we are not going to numb ourselves. We talked about anger as a "substitute", but any "emotional soothing" can be a quick reflexive "go to" action. What I noticed about myself was the more traumatic events kept stacking up in my life, the harder it was for me to push past that new batch of pain to even desire a level of clarity. Anything to numb me from the original source of pain and any accompanying self-inflicted guilt, embarrassment and deep regret. I was willing to use any emotional quick fix, because the emotional whirlwind, even without the anger, felt like it would steamroll over me. If, in these times, we ONLY TAKE CUES from those emotional demands, which I often did, then we remain out of control, detoured and off-course with what our life was designed to be.

Sometimes, the kind of unhealthy emotional accommodating I did can lead to very dark emotional outcomes and even physical pain cycles. Truthfully, it actually can lead us to a life of desolation, just like it did Tamar.

Emotional overindulgence does not work. Let me repeat that for the folks in the back! **<u>EMOTIONAL OVERINDULGENCE DOES NOT WORK!</u>** And neither does transient emotional soothing when the goal is obtaining healthy, emotionally balanced long-term results. No matter what is missing from our emotional scaffolding, the paths that do not offer us the bottom of the bottle are superficial and can potentially cause us to "waste our wisdom" and waste our lives.

Part of the reason for sharing this prescription is the hope that each of you will see yourself in the medicine I was able to extract from Tamar. If I can do it, there is no doubt we all can. We can do what we need to do, but we must REFUSE to settle for the status quo. One of the largest doses of this prescription I still take daily is the need to *keep my expectations leveled up, fight for clarity and refuse to leave without wisdom.*

Let us recap and reflect on where we are now. The path leading to this portion of the strategy is forgiveness, but the success of this strategy is locked in gaining the wisdom of the experience. We execute this plan with commitment and clarity, simple. Let's go further.

So, what is our part? We acknowledge our emotions, gain insight with healthy resources and assistance, and we make ourselves available for whatever is needed to recreate, repair, and rebuild the landscape of our life, considering what has occurred.

Up to this point, we have most of our prescription in hand and are more prepared to avoid what I call the "D" syndrome: depression, discouragement, destiny derailment and disease.

With this in mind, let us look back at the scripture for more strategy.

At the end of the horrific violation, the scripture tells us that Tamar was ejected from the home and the door bolted behind her. In short, she went to live in her brother Absalom's house as, what the Bible indicates, **a desolate woman**. Can you imagine how Tamar felt? Can you imagine what Tamar thought? In a culture where sexual purity was connected to family honor and wealth, can you imagine how the trajectory of her life shifted in one life event?

She was robbed of her innocence, her position, her ideals, her expectations. Her trust was broken, her body was violated, and the scripture says she lived in desolation.

What resonated with me in scripture was it did not describe her as having a season of sadness; the scripture says she lived in desolation. She lived fruitless and unproductive for the REST OF HER LIFE. Even though she did not expect to be raped, even though she did not ask to be raped, she did not deserve to be raped, it changed the way she lived.

Desolate. Was it because she could not forgive? Was it because she did not finish her "prescribed" bottle? Did she contract the "D" syndrome?

Well, the why behind her desolation is not spelled out in scripture, so we do not know. We also do not see any scriptural indication that she was offensively prepared. We cannot conclude, however, that she did not try to recover simply because she DID NOT recover. Our strategic observation is this: every effort may not lead us directly to recovery, but there is NO recovery without effort.

This next statement is rarely popular, but it is true, so hold on to your side posts and edges. The person hurt, the one damaged, the one most negatively impacted or victimized is the one that now has the responsibility to apply the effort to forgive, seek wisdom and heal. Yes, that is how it goes, and unfortunately, it is why most do not recover.

I hate to think of it, but we all know a Tamar. We all know someone, if it is not ourselves, who is stuck, reeling in the pain of a life "surprise." Crushed. Shamed. Alone. Depressed. One event. A marriage ends in bitter divorce and 10 years later, 30 years later, that corner of complete recovery has not been turned. So, what now?

If we only use objective measures, we'd be finished with this book. Tamar did not complete the path of recovery and she lived an unproductive life. The end. Dust your hands, grab your coat.

But that is so far from the end. What are the other fallouts when we do not recover? Any contribution she offered the culture, her community, her family was not realized. Her multi-million-dollar business idea never materialized, her social plans were never completed, she did not have children, she did not become an advocate for woman traumatized by sexual assault; the part of the "needle" she was responsible for did not move. She lived desolate.

Answer this, with all she had experienced, was she still responsible for fulfilling her life's assignment? The answer: yes, she was!

That is just it. In addition to applying the effort to heal and accessing the grace to move forward with a new and wiser perspective, she was also still responsible to complete her assignment. AND SO ARE WE.

We will not know what could have become of Tamar because she, like so many of us, got trapped in pain and ended up riding in vehicles of poverty, bitterness, emptiness, cynicism, sarcasm, or personal disassociation, becoming powerless servants to the pain that came to serve us.

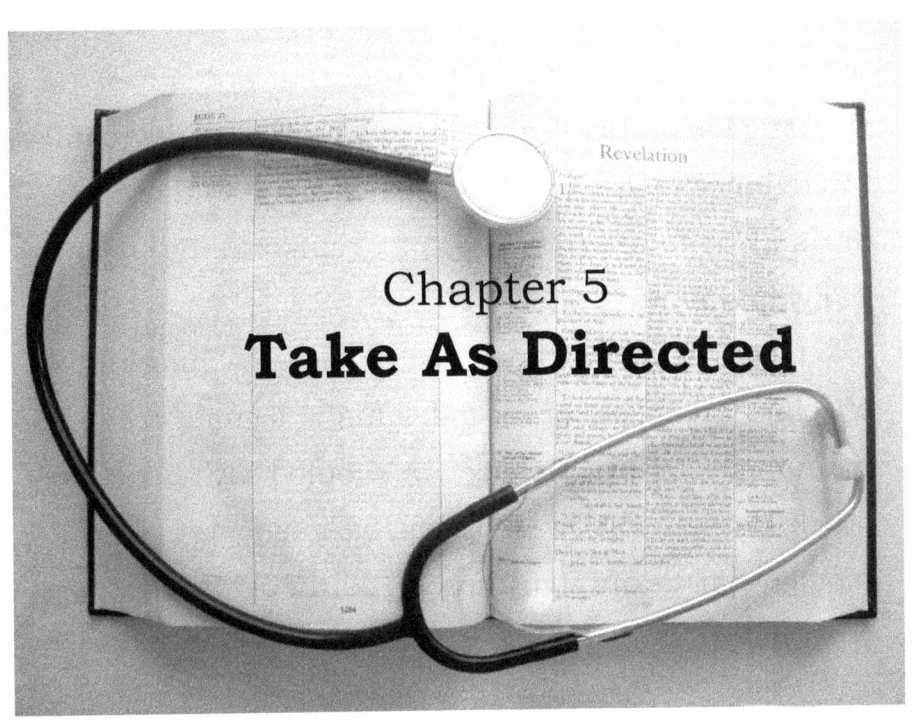

Chapter 5
Take As Directed

Purpose

The next piece of this prescription is a brief but powerful one designed to target this very issue. What is purpose? Do we have assignments to complete? Do we have reasons why we are here? Absolutely. It is the single word that gives life an irresistible push. Yes, we all have purpose, especially those that are citizens of the Kingdom of Heaven; we have a responsibility to our interconnected lives with other Believers, to those who are still bound by sin and, most importantly, to our individual purpose.

Our personal choices have wide-reaching ripple effects because our individual significance is monumental. Until we reject, or should I say refuse, the stuck, desolate life as an option, we may never gain the momentum to pursue purpose. Without purpose, we are surely at risk of things ending the way they did with TAMAR.

The good news is we have unlimited access to His strength; when we are hurting, we can choose to "take this prescription" and all the resources of Heaven and recover fully. We always have access to celebrate our unbroken fellowship and we are partakers of His authority through Jesus Christ. His love Never fails. To this point, I want to add this to the prescription: recovering is winning and winning is a choice. Repeat this: I CHOOSE TO WIN, BECAUSE I WAS DESIGNED TO WIN AND MY LIFE HAS PURPOSE.

In this new light, purpose becomes the ingredient that adds the refreshing water we need to win over tragedy. Purpose is God's stabilizing core. We can access it as a source of strength and direction when our lives are shattered into pieces because purpose remains intact under pressure. Purpose is what adds value and fuels resilience when we have known tremendous pain.

We already know nothing puts pressure on our mind and emotions like disappointment, frustration, and shame. One gateway to exiting that pressure is for us to respond back by applying a stronger opposing force called purpose. Of course, there is pressure to give up on relationships when we are attacked. Yes, there is pressure to give up when we are wounded. There is a huge push to stop caring about others when we have been betrayed. So, God gave us purpose and its unyielding nudges to use against that "give up" force.

Purpose is also a principle that that bridges all humanity because we are all born with and for purpose. The purpose of our lives is so powerful. Psalm 33:11 describes it as the entity that prevails.

> ***Psalm 33:11***
>
> *But the plans of the LORD stand firm forever, the purposes of his heart through all generations.*

Purpose, by definition then, opposes those things that oppose us and can be used to bring us to overcoming. Purpose is resistant. Purpose is strong. When we live in purpose and understand and embrace this stabilizing concept before a traumatic event, we create a landscape to maximize purpose as a resource for recovery when we need it.

Doesn't that make sense? Purpose can carry us with fury and fire through all of life's difficulties **_IF_** we are committed to fulfilling it. So that commitment to fulfilling purpose must be forged beforehand. When we use purpose as an offensive guard post, fulfilling purpose becomes the method we can use to ensure pain compensates us, and that is wonderful news!

We have individual purposes, and we have collective purpose. Commitment to both is better than commitment to either alone. Collectively, we are the salt of the Earth, we are Heaven's ambassadors. We are His mouthpieces and servant leaders to use for advancement of the Kingdom.

We are His replicas in this Earth. We mirror His image and likeness in EVERY situation. We have been placed on Earth as **CHRIST**ian Believers to tell those who are captive by sin that He is a liberating, loving God. Our contribution as Kingdom ambassadors has eternal implication and we are extremely necessary.

We also have a real delineated, specific personal purpose. We are not randomly selected or placed geographically, physically, or emotionally.

We have been entrusted with the responsibility of surrendering to this individual plan no matter what we encounter. Commitment to purpose is a must have.

Think of Jesus in the Garden of Gethsemane. His larger purpose was being fulfilled. He had developed a team of disciples that were going to continue to teach the new covenant Gospel long after He ascended to Heaven. People were being converted and accepting the new way of fellowship with God the

Father, and all of this did not preclude His commitment to His personal assignment.

This also did not excuse Him from the agony of humiliation and gossip. He was accused of being satan himself and ostracized by a large part of the elite religious leaders, and He still committed to His personal assignment.

Just like Jesus, we are not called to ignore our pain. The scripture says He set joy before Him in order to endure.

> **Hebrews 12:2**
>
> *Looking unto Jesus the author and finisher of our faith; who for the joy that was set before him endured the cross, despising the shame, and is set down at the right hand of the throne of God.*

The word endure implicitly points to the difficulty of the situation. Just as He endured, so should we. We do have the ability to endure hardships if we decide to do it. We have unlimited access to supernatural resources: strength, determination, relentlessness; they will all yield us as winners, if decided to use them.

I am driving this point home to reiterate the key idea of pre-set commitment to purpose. We must commit to live in purpose, on purpose. Purpose is offensive. Purpose is a strategy for winning because it inherently gives us a reason to recover and a reason to persevere. Purpose prompts us to use its force to forgive and love, because when we are weakened by betrayal, purpose is not. Purpose helps us. It is a gift that fuels a refusal to die unproductive. Purpose has the power within it to prevail.

So yes, we can take on a life of purpose and design in order to overcome. Let us look at overcoming in practical terms. Here is the largest part of the prescription so far. If we are going to decide against living in desolation, to get unstuck, there must also be a decision to BE FULLY ALIVE.

Tamar lived but living in desolation clearly is not being fully alive. There must be a decision to accept life for what it really is and live fully. This prescription was designed to be used to build or rebuild a life that can accommodate richness, fullness, joy and fulfillment without respect to life's pain and disappointments.

The rebuilding process, to be quite honest, is customizable. Which simply states the obvious, we are all different, so our rebuilds will all be different. There are some broad generalizations: for instance, disconnecting from anything or anyone who promotes long, unhealthy emotional resolve and intentionally reconnecting to people and places who encourage maturity, growth and insight. We disconnect to reconnect to our future hopes and ideas, keeping in mind, in order to live fully we must acknowledge, the main power source if all contentment is God Himself. There is also a huge component of trust to consider when rebuilding, especially if our ability to trust has been wounded. Deciding to live can be formidable because this level of living is a DECISION. Prior to some trauma and pain, we take living fully for granted. While most people have ambitions, goals, etc., not often are we faced with building a full life with INTENTIONAAL effort we're discussing until there is a life event that opposes the very thing we were passively seeking. In these instances, living a full life considers and embraces all the difficulty and pain we have discussed and more, but always know God is waiting to instruct us how to live abundantly in the face of it.

No one can prepare fully for the unexpected, so we must live wisely."
– Cyrene' Wright, MD

So many things in life pivot on the axis of perspective and living fully after trauma and disappointment are no different. When we live ready to forgive, understand wisdom hides in the unexpected places of life. When we commit to purpose and decide to live fully, we will see recovery as the opportunity it is.

As Kingdom citizens, we actually get the opportunity to expect to recover fully AND to recover well. With that expectation set, we need to use the resources from the Word of God as our foundation… resources like faith, unlimited access to God's power through His Word, fellowship and unconditional love. These are irrefutable supernatural resources that cannot fail when used well. Success is guaranteed when we do recovery God's way: through His Word and by His Wisdom.

The Kingdom principles of recovery are given as commands… commands that are not based on any circumstance happening to us These commands are instructions that urge us to commit to "happen back" to our circumstances. We get to embrace truth, we get to embrace freedom, we get to recover, we get to be KINGDOM!

When we can fully embrace Kingdom truth, we can embrace its freedom.

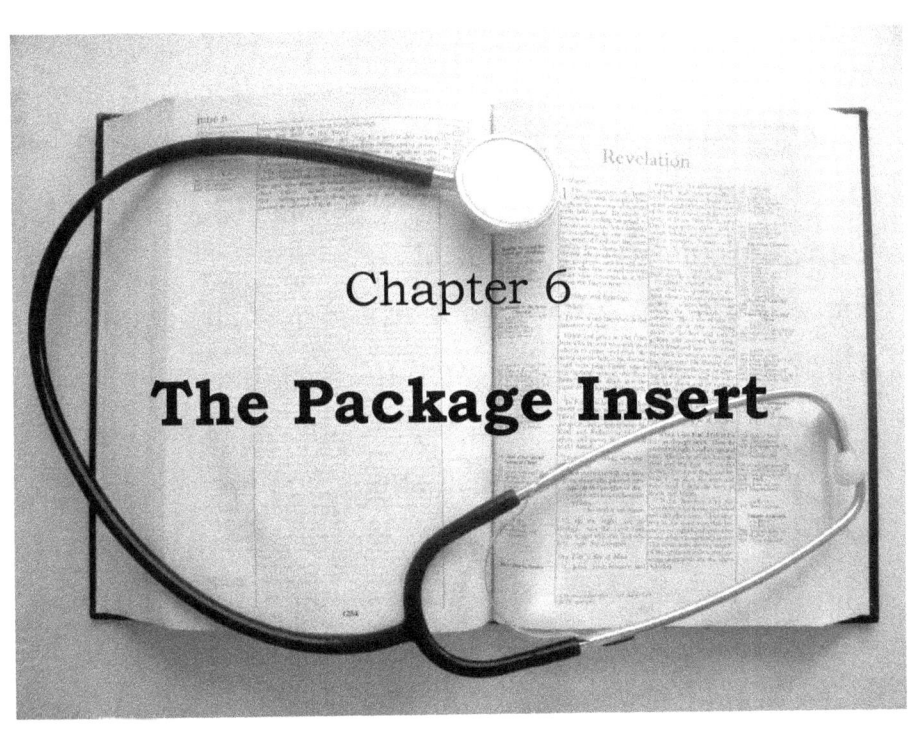

Chapter 6

The Package Insert

Package Inserts

John 16:13 - Howbeit when He, the Spirit of truth, is come, He will guide you into all truth: for He shall not speak of Himself; but whatsoever He shall hear, that shall He speak: and He will shew you things to come.

To prepare as students of life, even for our own experiences, we must be willing and ready to be taught. Once I became an adult, I decided or perhaps I extracted this idea from social cues, but I realized how much I did not know about living the life I wanted. There are so many things we must admit we simply do not know. The humility of this simple admission was the catalyst for most of my sustainable progress. In my personal experience and in my experience with others, especially those that are professionally successful or academically advantaged, I find a huge barrier to the simple humility of admitting 'I do not know how to get out of this.'

The Bible tells us that we should teach and admonish one another with psalms, hymns, and spiritual songs (Colossians 3:16). This scripture shows us a connection between us being taught or illuminated in our understanding by the Holy Spirit of God.

There is an indelible line that goes directly from the Holy Spirit, who is the Comforter and Teacher, and our ability, capacity and willingness to learn. It is so crucially important that we be willing to allow the Spirit of the Lord to guide us as a Teacher when life has moments of disappointment. "Devastation places" can be overwhelmingly painful and bewildering, so allowing the Holy Spirit to teach us is the best way to ensure that our lessons will be learned well.

When emotions are high and experiences are raw, there is no more opportune time than this to be guided by the Holy Spirit. Pain can be a distraction to the promptings of the Holy Spirit. Pain and anguish, once we have properly allowed ourselves to experience it in a healthy way, can also point us to an opportunity to learn.

The Kingdom key is that we let the Holy Spirit, do the teaching. Let us look at Matthew 28:19-20. This scripture shows us the connection between wisdom and the past.

Matthew 28:19-20

¹⁹ Go ye therefore, and teach all nations, baptizing them in the name of the Father, and of the Son, and of the Holy Ghost:

²⁰ Teaching them to observe all things whatsoever I have commanded you: and, lo, I am with you always, even unto the end of the world. Amen.

This does not suggest pain is the **only way** to gain wisdom; that is absolutely NOT TRUE. What we are saying is this, when pain shows up unexpectedly, do not leave that season without the lesson and its wisdom. It is essential to embrace the lessons in tragedy as we have discussed in the previous section. We are now highlighting the fact that the Holy Spirit is the teacher.

How we learn and who we learn from are as pivotal to learning as being humble enough to become a student. When our view on life is built on suspicion and mistrust, we will find "life" learning difficult. When we have settled for bitterness and personal transient vindication, we will find learning difficult. If our view is skewed by social ills or economic structures, we may likely not learn well. We learn from the Holy Spirit and from fellowship with Him in order to bring clarity of thought into the process. The Holy Spirit is committed to guide us in truth.

Chapter 7
Caution:
Federal Law Prohibits...

What are boundaries? Boundaries are guidelines, rules or limits a person creates to identify reasonable, safe, and permissible ways for other people to behave towards them, **before** any unexpected events occur. When we started this prescription, we talked about unexpected events. Things in life that cause trauma, betrayals, any hurtful or tragic event we never saw coming. We moved from there to talk about what we can choose to learn AFTER this type of experience. How wisdom can be trapped in the core of unwanted experiences – so we have to finish the bottle. Which brings us here: discussing the consummate offensive strategy for every unexpected: boundaries.

Living with personal boundaries as an offensive strategy is how we make safe choices for ourselves, beforehand. These are choices we make and commit to keep, because they have shown to keep us or others safe.

Now safe has many contextual definitions. The safety included in a boundary can be to keep someone safe from being wrongly accused, or a boundary to prevent unnecessary exposure to crime or sicknesses. There are also boundaries that keep professional workplaces safe. The safety feature of boundaries is relative, but the principle of boundaries is universal.

There is an element of vulnerability in life that is unescapable. Let us settle into that. Boundaries are still necessary because they create offensive safeguards that work to protect us when protection is possible.

This is why we have emphasized throughout the prescription that we are not to blame or assess judgment of another person reaction or inability to act in the moment. In fact, if we have experienced situations where we could not keep ourselves self from assault, attack or abuse, we are clear blaming is not our springboard.

Like an advocate for children's safety who speaks with passion on how to prevent your child from the horrors their own children may have faced, we are allowing TAMAR to 'speak' to us from the walls of scripture as our safety advocate. Encouraging us to consider boundary principles that were not recorded in her scriptural account.

More to the point, this is how Holy Spirit explained this concept for me. Boundaries were and still are a hugely important part of what I had to learn about how to keep myself form feeling continually victimized. As we build personal strategies, real boundaries also have nestled within them the type and character of the response to be associated with any interaction that violates that boundary.

The safe relationship piece was so important for me because I was ignorant to how this wisdom could highlight red flags that were waving right in from of my face. I honestly did not know the process of keeping myself safe.

Keeping this in mind, as crucial as boundaries are to maintaining safe relationships, they are not impenetrable. Boundaries will not PREVENT unexpected experiences of life. Scripture very clearly points to this truth "life happens to every man." And there has not been a man (woman) that has not had life happen. This reality also does not mean we should be naively exposed and unwisely vulnerable, the way I was for many years. What I want to highlight here is this: we have the opportunity within this prescription to decide to acknowledge the reality of potential harm. As well as dismiss the fallacy that life has a duty to be anything other than life.

When I initially acknowledged this about life, it seemed a bit discouraging. But the maturing of my perspective was eventually its own reward. We need to come to terms with the mature truth that life has disappointments. Deep disappointments. Let us take a quick look at how the scripture prepares us for the realities of life.

Ecclesiastes 9:11, *(CEV)*

Here is something else I have learned: The fastest runners and the greatest heroes don't always win races and battles. Wisdom, intelligence, and skill don't always make you healthy, rich, or popular. We each have our own share of misfortune.

John 16:33 (AMPC)

I have told you these things, so that in Me you may have [perfect]
peace and confidence. In the world you have tribulation and trials and distress and frustration; but be of good cheer [take courage; be confident, certain, undaunted]! For I have overcome the world. [I have deprived it of power to

harm you and have conquered it for you.]

OK it is settled, life **will** happen, but we **will** be positioned in the offensive with forgiveness, wisdom and boundaries.

Here is our last instruction about boundaries. Even when life surprises us with unwelcomed and hugely impactful curve balls, personal boundaries, by definition, always remain within our control. This empowers us by having us to know, even we fully honored our boundaries we have done everything that was within our control to avoid the situation. This springboard can help us recover from the parts of the situation that were clearly out of our control. When we think about our spiritual context, Tamar never recovered. But that is far too common when we are caught off guard and spin emotionally out of control. When we are out of control, we are unsafe, we are panicked, and we are unable to gain clarity or self-regulate. When we cannot interrupt this cycle of emotional chaos, we can have trouble with our recovery. I say this because it is exact cycle of emotional hydroplaning I found myself in far too often;

thus, boundary setting has become the flagship of my passion. Boundaries are designed to help us re-establish emotional safety, after our safety has been disrupted.

As we excavate Tamar's experience in the context of boundaries, we will extrapolate areas where boundary principles can be found. Clearly this is not an exhaustive list of boundaries, as real boundaries are based on an individual's personal limits. These are the boundaries Holy Spirit inspired me to write from scripture as a kick start. Full transparency, I really needed to learn the basics of how to keep myself relationally safe for and in all relationships. I had operated in self-sabotaging obligation for so long; these fundamental "starters" were the thrust I needed to step in the right direction. Since then, I have grown personally and cultivated additional boundaries that fit my life and my personal goals. This part is the ultimate "take away," of this prescription. building our own customized personal boundaries. Together with knowing the strength needed to honor these boundaries are available for us in the WORD of God, we are well on our wat to heal and recover.

Here are a few tips to help you get started establishing boundaries in any relationship:

- Be clear in your thoughts about why they exist – this could be a personal preference, a health concern or wisdom from someone else's experience.
- Be honest but respectful when sharing your boundaries with other people. Be firm and proactive. Do not avoid the discussion.
- Never assume or guess someone knows your boundaries. Making assumptions can create misunderstandings. You may feel like you know a person well enough to avoid the discussion However, it is never good to assume.
- Follow through on what you say. Setting boundaries and not executing them allows people to think they can continue to overstep your boundaries. You should not make any exceptions. If necessary, rethink the boundary and change it if needed. You do not want to communicate to yourself it is ok to be unsafe.
- Take responsibility for your actions. Instead of immediately blaming others, take a step back

and think about the choices you have made and take responsibility for it.
- Know when it is time to move on. Persistent disregard for boundaries is a sign of a larger underlying problem. You are not responsible for your partner's feelings to the point that you should tolerate being disrespected. When people will not respect your boundaries, then it may be time to end the relationship.

Setting and establishing healthy boundaries is an acquired skill that takes time to cultivate! Remember, healthy boundaries do not come easy, but if you trust your Holy Spirit led instincts, be open, and practice sharing them, then your relationships will only get stronger over time.

Let's get started. Let us investigate a few boundary principals that could have impacted Tamar's interaction with Amnon.

Boundary Principle #1
Authority-Driven Directives
2 Samuel 13:10
"Then Amnon said to Tamar, "**Bring the food into the bedroom, so that I may eat from your hand.**" So,

Tamar took the cakes she had made and brought them into the bedroom to her [half-] brother Amnon."

David (Tamar's father and the current King of Israel) had given his daughter directions to go to her brother's house and cook for him because he was not feeling well. David's directive was clear and direct. This is what spurns our first boundary. Countless situations require us to take directions from others. Simply put, when we are given a set of reasonable directives to adhere to by an entity of authority, follow them!

Boundaries must be set up concerning even this simple circumstance. However, when an adjustment needs to be made to an original set of authoritative directives, those adjustments should be given by the person that gave the original directive.

This seems like a very simple boundary and one that might be easy to disregard, but this is a huge point of safety and wisdom. Research concerning sexual assaults by known perpetrators indicates that 57% of those victimized had a directive change at the last minute that caused them to be susceptible. If people are hoping to deceive or distract us, one simple method to create diversion is by changing directives in the middle of a task.

This particular boundary works in most any relational context and can be simply adhered to by being willing to make this idea clear at the beginning of the exchange. It is equally appropriate to address any changes in given directives as they arise. Simply put, nothing changes without all parties being aware.

A quick verification about new directives will unlikely be a problem for a person with no adverse agenda. This boundary is highly effective in covering misrepresented characters and keeps all focus on the initial goal. This simple boundary is powerful and effective.

The fact that the original instructions came from King David would have made this seemingly menial task easy to follow and uneventful in maintaining this boundary. Firstly, the King was her father. She had a relationship with him and could have easily gotten clarity about the changes Amnon was making. Tamar could have relied on her familial relationship to gain clarity about what Amnon requested versus what the king told her to do.

When we need to enforce our boundaries, we can look for relationships that will offer us support. Our objective in clarifying new instructions should not take on the context of being paranoid or suspicious of other people per se. Much to the contrary, it should be done with the only objective of following orders and maintaining a safe space.

In this and each scenario we will discuss, we cannot afford to be talked out of our boundaries. Boundary-keeping can be plagued with the daunting thought of being offensive to the other person. When we construct boundaries, however, we must reinforce them with one thought: these are the kinds of things I do to help keep me safe, and my priority is my own personal safety.

Boundary Principle #2

Minimize Assumptions

2 Samuel 13:11

"When she brought them to him to eat, he took hold of her and said, **'Come, lie with me, my sister.'**"

The boundary we can extrapolate from this verse is one that was broken by implication. He asked his sister to come and lie with him, which in today's language is a request for a sexual encounter. Of course, this is unacceptable. So, it follows that Tamar refused Amnon's request. There is an obvious boundary around incestuous relationships. Siblings should not have intimate relationships. What is not so obvious, however, is the more insidious assumption on behalf of Amnon. Amnon assumed Tamar would think this was an acceptable idea.

It is a clear and reasonable boundary to reject the assumption from people you align with things that are wholly inappropriate.

As we have stated, Amnon had devised a scheme to have sex with his sister. To that end, he asked her to bring the food in his room and feed him. However, when she went into the room, he said to her, "Come lie down with me and let's have sex." Now the ill-conceived notion was and will forever be outrageous from all perspectives.

Even worse, the gross presumption that she would have sex with him was more outrageous. He assumed that once he tricked her into coming into his room, she would be agreeable to the suggestion to have incestuous sex with her brother. The boundary emerges when we realize how important it is to express limits in relationships when the other party makes assumptions about you.

For Amnon, to assume Tamar would be agreeable with his plan is alarming at best. We assert that he thought she would agree because after she denied his request, he forced her. That was the ultimate violation, however, we recognize the preceding boundary violation is also notable.

One way we can avoid instances that bring about bad assumptive conclusions is to acknowledge the intent and character of people in our lives, especially family. We know familial relationships may not have the same value and meaning to other people as they do to us. There are some family members that are willing to violate, betray, deceive, and disrespect anyone, including and ESPECIALLY their family members.

When people make assumptions about us and our character so that it is more aligned with the projections of their character, this should send up a huge red flag as well as be the foundational basis in creating an important boundary. We should create boundaries around our relationships that do not permit assumptions about who we are, what we will do, and what we will accommodate. These are issues that should be discussed, and all decisions should be clear between both parties. When we are prepared to make paths for healthy relationships, we will not allow assumptions to be made about us.

Boundary Principle #3

Create a Safe Space

2 Samuel 13:12a

"She replied, **_No, my brother!_** Do not force *and* humble me,"

It is vital to establish personal safety. Most often we find that we can make assumptions about people that cause us to relax on our criteria for relationships. This happens very easily amongst family members and this is the context for this boundary.

Understand that it *appeared* that all roads were leading to Tamar being threatened with an impending sexual assault, but all doubts were removed by the time we reached 2 Samuel 12 when she realized Amnon's intentions to violate her. He suggested that she willingly participate but because it was incestuous and dishonorable, she, of course, objected. Yet amid this ordeal, she continued to refer to him as brother.

This could have been a reference of geographical familiarity. It could have been a reference of Kingdom relationship. It could have been a reference of posterity because she had known him for a long time but in fact, he was her half- brother, both having King David as their father. The fact of the matter was that Tamar was unwilling to accept Amnon's breach of family honor. She continued to refer to him as brother instead of acknowledging he was the person that desired to violate her.

When establishing boundaries to protect our space and peace, we must realize that family must be included in people who are subjected to these boundaries. A sibling, grandmother, uncle, nephew, daughter, husband should not be automatically included in a safe space when they have demonstrated, without question, that they are willing to violate the standards of our character.

We position ourselves in the wisdom of safety when we recognize this fact. Family members are not exempt from the lessons on boundaries that we can extract from this scripture. We must be prepared to see people for who they are at that moment and then begin to take action to guard ourselves.

When we are prepared to safeguard ourselves, we will not be easily distracted by the relationship we have with the person. Clearly Tamar's efforts to help her half-brother are understandable on its face. This was her half-brother. However, once she realized his intentions were to harm her, to demean her, to shame her, to utterly humiliate her, Tamar was face-to-face with an opportunity to rescue herself with a strong personal boundary. When clearly defined boundaries are in place, they should apply to everyone and will operate most effectively when we are willing to make the requirements for relationship without faltering.

We do recognize that family relationships are crucially important, and we are not in any way suggesting that we dismiss familial relationships and their significance. In the same way, we must hold ourselves accountable to our own safety by substituting an inferred relationship (because we have the same parents) with the reality of the devastation and chaos that is brought into the atmosphere by the person.

Without question, family members are used more than strangers to deceive and trick people, because it is often unimaginable to believe that a family member is the one who would carry out this atrocity. However, we clearly see in the scripture that her brother had devised this plan and was very intentional in carrying it out.

This is a stark reality we must come to and give complete credence to when creating a boundary to protect our space. Regrettably, we learn from our experience that family will hurt us and can be influenced to mistreat and betray us. Thus, they must be required to meet the same standard of relationship. This is a MUST.

Boundary Principle #4
Create Realistic Expectations
2 Samuel 13:12b
"For no such thing should be <u>done in Israel!</u> Do not do this foolhardy, scandalous thing!"

This verse of scripture shows a boundary around people in personal relationships like the ones we previously discussed. This boundary is similar to the previous one however, the impact of not keeping this boundary has the potential to cause more damage due to the implied expectation for this level of spiritual authority and leadership. The difference between the previous and this current boundary is Tamar's expectation of integrity based on the history of the children of Israel and the region being in covenant with God.

Tamar began to plead in a time of potential harm, that her attacker recalls the history of integrity of the region and its people. This is like what happened in modern day churches.

Far too often we relax boundaries around people's intentions or their methods simply because they attend or have a "position" in church. We create unsafe personal engagements with people presumptuously because of the expectation we have set around a physical church and its inhabitants.

Now this is not to say there should be no expectations in a church environment, however, expectations that are based merely on someone arriving at a building where church service is held weekly is nothing short of dangerous.

In general, people have a conjecture of appropriate behavior regarding the church; they expect "church folks" to do right 100% of the time, without any room for error. In short, they need to see perfection. Anything short of flawlessness is unacceptable.

This is where many people become disappointed with the Church because of these erroneous expectations. Yes, the "Church" should live a holy and blameless life. Yes, the "Church" should serve God and live a life that displays the character of Christ: honest, trustworthy, full of love, bearing compassion, granting mercy and helping those in need. God forbid if the "Church" steps outside of these boundaries.... the backlash and judgement that ensues is merciless.

The irony is that the expectations they hold of the "Church" they do not hold for themselves. What some people fail to realize is that we as Christians are imperfect people, serving a perfect God who is transforming us day by day to be more like Him. People do not allow much time for the process to proceed!

Tamar, in much the same way, had an expectation of her brother and father. After she referred to Amnon as brother and made every attempt to have him reconsider his actions based on their familial disposition, she then tried to appeal to his loyalty to God and their nation. In essence, Tamar was saying "we are God's chosen people; this will be a source of shame against the God of Israel." She is suggesting Amnon's status with the holy nation of Israel should be a boundary against his inappropriate behavior.

It is not unusual for us to have expectations that certain behavior is unacceptable among people that have a relationship with the King of Kings. We are not wrong to think people will honor the presence of God, the house of God, the principles of God, however we do run the risk of having our expectations disappointed when we do not recognize that amongst the people that are in a body of Believers, there are those who will have no regard for how their behavior impacts them, us or reflects on our God. This is the essence of the boundary that we create from this view of Tamar's interaction with Amnon.

It is unwise to make the supposition implied in this verse, in that the expectation can set unachievable behavior and resulting trauma. We must have a safe understanding about people in in the body of Christ that are in leadership or have a position of title and authority in a local church. To assume they will automatically honor that position is dangerous.

The element of boundaries that keeps us safe is not only that we set them but also determine how we will act when they are violated. It is clear that to Tamar, this act was not only atrocious but should also be not named among the people of God. She revered Amnon's and her position as the chosen people of God and felt that her brother should have had enough respect for God to self-govern and behave appropriately. Tamar tried to negotiate with her attacker on a principle she had expected. We are never safe when we make assumptions of expected behavior. We are never safe when we operate based on presumptions that are being proven to be untrue. Once people make their intentions clear, we have the opportunity to make decisions about these people to keep ourselves safe.

Tamar had placed much more value on her expectation of Amnon's spirituality than on what was potentially going to happen to her. This also translates to how some of our expectations can work against us when we have not set them to include healthy boundaries. We must be prepared to resolve that, although some level of expectation should, in fact, be placed on those who carry a title in church leadership, the totality of their behavior should include title/position and the integrity of said title. Very rarely do two people have an exact duplicate set of values and beliefs; do not presume anyone's value system is the same as yours. Instead, we should create relational boundaries that have enough grace to accommodate anyone whose perspective is different from ours.

We all know assumptions are never a safe component of any relationship, however, we can mistakenly create "default" expectations in a church that we would not make in any other public setting. For example, if we do generalize about behavioral expectations in a workplace, we are generally not emotionally crushed or assign any blame to God when people do not meet those expectations. We oftentimes have a default expectation of character and integrity in the setting of a local church and are subsequently wounded by and negatively impacted when the people in that Body do not meet that expectation.

For this boundary to be clear and effective, we must decide that everyone in the local church is seeking more of God to bring balance to whatever areas in their life they do not reflect the image of God. With that understanding, we cannot interact freely with people in the local whose unacceptable behavior and lack of respect for the God of that same church is evident.

Lastly, within the same boundary, when it is obvious that a person is not regarding the God of their salvation, we must decide to keep ourselves emotionally and, if necessary, psychologically and physically safe. This boundary prevents us from the assumptive danger that because we are all children of God, we are all going to behave accordingly.

Tamar was aware that this should have been the case, however, we can decide that when we recognize people in the house of God that are not safe to be around, we remove ourselves.

Depending on the level of danger and the toxic nature of the circumstance, we may need to separate ourselves quickly, and in some instances permanently, to help avoid the possible pitfalls of the alternative.

Boundary Principle #5

Trust What You See

2 Samuel 13:12b

"Do not do this foolhardy, scandalous thing!"

To put it in the words of a widely popular adage, "I have come to learn that when people show us who they are the first time, believe them."

Tamar, as we have previously discussed, first used familial relationship and then she used a relationship to God to attempt to deflect the determination of Amnon not to violate her. As much as we are learning safe personal boundaries from the interaction of these two characters, we realize that Tamar also had the opportunity to recognize Amnon's behavior when his conversation and character were indicating his intentions.

It is a safe position to listen keenly to what a person says or watch intently to discover what a person's behavior says about their character. One is not considered a great person of faith if, however, they choose to look past the clear signs of unpalatable spiritual, physical, mental, emotional, social and even financial behavior, as if they have not seen what was clearly on display; there is no badge of honor if people continue to extend "grace" to the reckless violators without establishing protective boundaries. When we establish healthy boundaries, we are creating relationship dynamics that cannot easily cause misunderstandings when enforced. More importantly, when we ignore who people show themselves to be, we are lying to ourselves by omission of an actual occurrence.

This pathway to self-deception is oftentimes not uncovered until a person does something that is overtly damaging, and, in a reflective moment, we determine we have, in fact, known this about the person's character for a very long time. Self-deception in relationships is a clear violation of any boundary. If relationships imply that self-deception is required, if we feel obligated to ignore the reality of a person to have a relationship with them, or if someone suggests that we ignore what we have observed about a person to benefit from a relationship, we are violating boundaries that would help keep us safe.

In my opinion, this boundary is most empowering yet the most often ignored because the enforcement of the boundary relies on the individual's willingness to be honest with themselves about what they know of the other person. Relationships that have benefits (i.e., job promotions or business opportunities) can easily tempt us to ignore what we have seen about the person to get and maintain benefits. Very rarely are the benefits of the relationship going to outweigh the devastation associated with self-deception.

We must remind ourselves that boundaries in relationships are created to maintain the integrity of the interaction and the safety of both individuals. In reality, this type of self-deception is an interpersonal betrayal and can leave us in deeper emotional despair because it can potentially erode self-confidence and cause a mistrust inwardly.

This area of relational engagement must be taken seriously to avoid creating damage in the relationship we have with ourselves. This idea may seem like a non-urgent priority however the essence of enforcing personal boundaries is based on the integrity of the relationship we have with ourselves. If this boundary has been previously eroded, it can be self-perpetuating to continue ignoring evidence of a person's actions and character.

Boundary Principle #6

Demeaning Tones and Defaming Words

2 Samuel 13:15

"Then Amnon hated her exceedingly, so that his hatred for her was greater than the love with which he had loved her. And Amnon said to her, **Get up and get out!**"

As we have already stated, what makes events tragic or hugely impactful with negative outcomes is the reality that these events are unscheduled and unexpected. Tamar, at the direction of her father King David, had simply gone to her brother's home to assist him because he was not feeling well and was suddenly facing a violent incestuous sexual assault.

Scripture states that as soon as Amnon finished the atrocious sexual assault, all the enamored, infatuated feelings of love he had for Tamar was now a deep, heinous hatred. He then said to her "get up and get out." Clearly in this instance, Tamar did not have a chance or prayer of having any interactions prior to this to engage and gain insight about who he was, however we can still develop a boundary from how this could apply to us in modern-day relationships.

In looking to extrapolate present-day boundaries from Tamar's past, we must be willing to measure people's reactions during interpersonal exchanges. Measure is defined as estimates or assessments of the extent, quality, value, or effect of something. This may serve more as a red flag to someone that would violate a boundary, but it is a powerful point to make, nonetheless. When we are engaging people, we must create boundaries around how we will speak, the tone a conversation can take, and the safety of conversations within the context of the relationship. To that end, when engaging people, we must be aware of how they say what is said.

Closely look at the process of the manipulative scheme Amnon carried out against Tamar. What is important to note is not only his arrogant and dismissive position concerning her but also the language and words that were documented to represent what he said. Word choice and tone suggested how he felt about Tamar and for us to remain safe, the text and tone cannot be ignored.

Make no mistake. It matters how a person speaks to us, the tone they use, the words they select, and how they are willing to carry out their thoughts towards us; all is crucially important and a boundary that must be adhered to for this boundary. The suggestion that Amnon would violate Tamar then put her out is disgraceful. For him to "say get up and get out" indicates his utter disrespect and disregard for her.

We have the privilege of the studying this text thousands of years later with great insight and thus realize that Amnon's "passions" for his half-sister were reversed once he fulfilled his fantasy. He thought it not robbery to project his regret onto her and bring lifelong shame from his actions.

From Amnon and Tamar, we can easily see that relationships must have boundaries around communication. There is not only the deep need for communication but also an imperative need of consistent communication to maintain the safety of both people and the integrity of the partnership. We must not be afraid to measure what and how a person says, especially if the expectation is for a healthy interaction. The quickest way to recognize the context of any life relationship is to acknowledge and measure words and reactions as we engage with the person.

Boundary Principle #7
Boldly Protect Your Peace
2 Samuel 13:16

"But she said, No! This great evil of sending me away is worse than what you did to me. But he would not listen to her."

In verse 16 of the same chapter, we see where Tamar began to make a refusal and a plea. The text implies that when she initially heard of Amnon's plan to put her out, she vehemently screams out because she was clear of the isolating and demoralizing consequences that she would have to live with for the rest of her life. What do we draw as a place to maintain our safety from this experience with Tamar? Always be ready to be bold and courageous when engaging with other people.

Why do we say bold and courageous? ... because it took a lot of courage for Tamar to refuse to be dismissed. After all, she had been violated and assaulted! She been tricked and she responded with a very bold refusal. As we can see from her previous dialogue the incestuous relationship was inappropriate, the sexual assault and violations was obviously inappropriate, but we see Tamar with a bold response in verse 16 where she injects a refusal to be further traumatized.

This is where we extract wisdom for the next boundary we will discuss. Verse 16 is the first-time scripture records Tamar showing absolute refusal to cooperate. She simply says... NO!

Let us begin by seeing how powerful the word "NO" is. Two small letters that transform nations, a word that stops world disasters and creates peace in the face of turmoil. NO! Just as simple as that. No is where ALL boundaries of any category start their formation!

Boundaries are an extension of our personal decision that a certain type of behavior is not acceptable. They are the explanation and guidelines for our "no" decisions in life. This concept connects us to the experience with Tamar because her previous dialogue suggested Ammon was violating her personal boundary. However, not until verse 16 did she say the word NO!

No, in instances of pending trauma and violation, must be said with clarity and boldness. Tamar leaves us with a great springboard to gain wisdom. When we are being threatened and our boundaries are being crossed, we must say NO loud and often. This may seem like a remedial directive, but it is pivotal. The actual word NO! is how we indicate to people they are not to go any further with a conversation, idea, or plan. It is our first defense of our personal, psychological and physical space and we must always be prepared in any situation to use it.

No is a power word! Simple. NO indicates you realize you have a choice and your willingness to confront anyone or anything that would suggest differently. Most instances of violation or disrespect are occasions to try and shame or humiliate us for using our personal authority to set boundaries. However, it remains true, NO! is the power place.

Now in a pure cultural context, it would have been disgraceful for Tamar to assert a boundary in that way, which may explain why she did not make the proclamation earlier, and from this we draw another significant point: we know the strength of our own personal constitutions when we are ready to defy cultural and societal norms to protect ourselves.

This is not to be confused with those that create a life of rebellion and anti-conformity for the sake of controversy; this point is being made to reinforce the idea that we are always self-empowered. We are always free to refuse to go along with any plan to do us harm. We must always be ready, bold, and courageous enough to say NO!

We must be ready to refuse to go along with what someone says when it only serves their interest while jeopardizing ours. We must be ready to take a stand for our principles and our personal constitution; we must be ready to make declarative refusals even when they go against the cultural norm. We must always be prepared to defend our personal space and our safety with boldness and courage.

Boundary Principle #8

Refuse to Be Manipulated

2 Samuel 13:16

But she said, No! **This great evil of sending me away is worse than what you did to me.** But he would not listen to her.

Do not allow yourself to become part of a manipulative scheme. Manipulation is a strategy used by anyone with the goal of controlling our thoughts and emotions, especially in the context of them being deceptive, disloyal or of low character.

This boundary is the one I am most grateful to Tamar for exposing through record of her dialogue with Amnon. I have found that manipulative strategies are a very common way that many uses to operate daily, especially when they have betrayed someone's trust or violated a relationship.

In the cultural context of the verses, it was a form of disapproval or punishment for a woman to be put out by her husband. The inference was that she was irresponsible or had done something to deserve this punishment. The punishment would be isolation from her social group, other women in the community, and the shame of disappointing her husband and her family. These were the types of punishments that were used for women that did not complete household chores properly, take care of the children, or did not meet the request made of her daily.

This is in part why Tamar objected so strongly to the suggestion that Amnon gave the servant to put her out and lock the door behind. The issue is, however, Amnon had sexually violated her and shamed her and then decided to create a scenario that made it appear as if she had done something wrong.

As we know from reading the text, she had simply followed the instructions of the king. She had done nothing wrong. We must realize that by refusing to be manipulated, we become part of a deceptive mirage which makes us an active participant in the hatred that motivated the manipulator in the beginning. We must refuse to be manipulated. We must refuse to partake in manipulative situations. We must hold people accountable and be unwilling to camouflage their wrongdoing, especially when the alternative would involve being honest with themselves and others.

Amnon not only wanted to have his hatred for Tamar intact but also wanted to create a scenario that would obviate him of his accountability in violating her. Tamar has given us a gift in showing us that in any relationship of life, we must be clear of our personal responsibility and hold the other parties in the partnership equally responsible.

If there is betrayal, disloyalty, miscommunication, or mistrust, each party must be honest and willing to take accountability and steer clear of manipulative stories that would explain away the circumstances. As we see, this boundary will keep us from being the recipient of a violent and vile agenda of the other person to hurt us and it will also keep us clear of that person side-stepping their accountability.

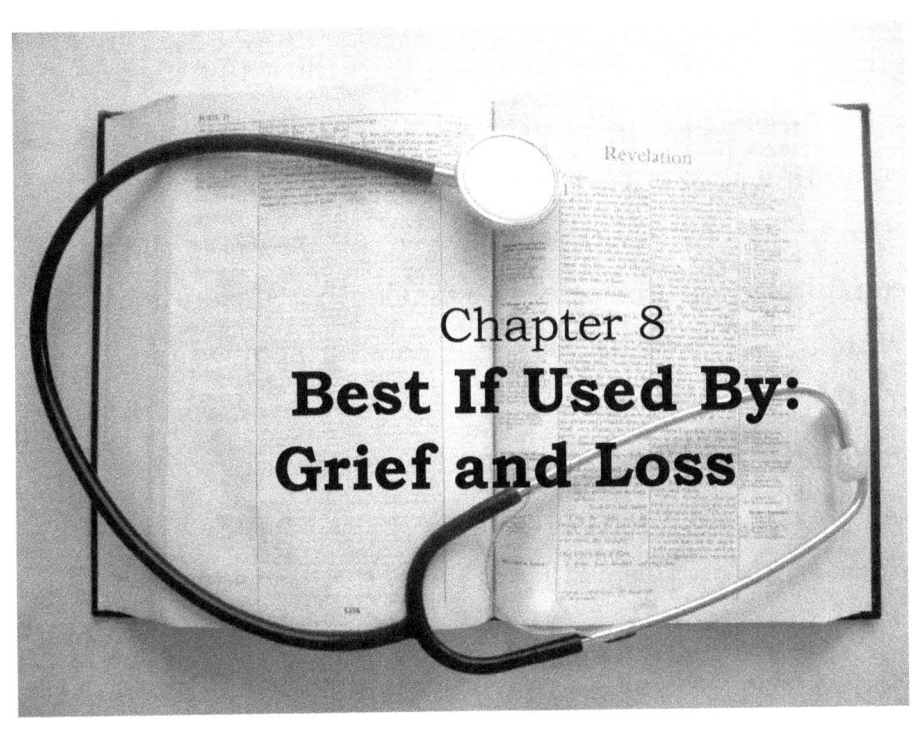

Chapter 8
Best If Used By: Grief and Loss

Grief & Loss

At the start of the previous section, we explained how most tragedies in life are unexpected. We took a closer look at Tamar's behavior for clues to create personal boundaries. The big picture up to this point has been how to create a step-by-step process, an offensive strategy to assist in weathering life's most unexpected events. This entire prescription hinges on a commitment to ourselves to have healthy engagements, a commitment to ourselves to be accountable and a commitment to ourselves to hold other accountable. Without fail. These personal commitments must be forged with boldness because we are now aware how vital relationships with healthy boundaries help us align with our bigger personal goals and fuel us to pursue our purpose with confidence and wisdom.

We went on to discuss the limitations of boundaries even around relationships and how boundaries can help create environments for relationships to grow and develop.

In the same way we use boundaries to create safe springboards for every type of relationship, if relationships are lost for any reason, we do ourselves a service if we are willing to acknowledge what was lost. We cannot attempt to ignore of minimize the expectations or hopes that have been dashed when things we could not have expected materialized.

Keep this point in mind, parts of this prescription are framed around relationships only because relationship trauma makes up a huge facet of the type of events we are addressing. But the idea of acknowledging a loss does not only apply to relationships. There is an appropriate level of introspection we should require of our hearts that allows us to admit we have suffered the loss of a relationship, or hope, or career, or friendship or whatever it is. Too often, we try gimmicks and popular sayings to bypass this painful but necessary step. However, to rebuild, reestablish and resolve, we must admit we have suffered a loss. This was so hard for me to do. I felt like a "loser." I was jealous of people that had not lost what I had lost, so I wanted to act as though it had not happened. But it did, and I had to acknowledge it, to heal.

Oh my, yes, there are many types of losses. That is why it is important to mention that loss of expectation and loss of a dream are as significant as loss of finances or loss of a home. We should not dismiss the loss of trust in a person as a real loss. Loss is loss. Trust in relationships and integrity among business partners are reasonable to expect and if they are not present or are betrayed, it should be acknowledged as a loss. Acknowledging our losses is the validation we need to declutter the path to reframing future expectations and rebuilding new relationships.

How do we acknowledge loss? One way is by having a <u>healthy</u> grieving season.

The scripture indicates to us that there is a time to grieve and moreover, those of us that are Kingdom citizens have a specific way, we are instructed to grieve. We are to grieve but not as though we have no hope (1 Thessalonians 4:13). How could the grieving process render us hopeless? To begin, one way is what we just discussed, our refusal to acknowledge what was lost. We can also be rendered hopeless if we are not willing to embrace transition and new possibilities. If we are overwhelmed with guilt, shame, and bitterness, these will negatively impact the grieving season and, quite frankly, every other phase of life moving forward from that time.

When we look at the biblical account of Tamar's grieving and study the original meaning of the words, we see that Tamar's grief morphed into bitterness. The scripture says she lamented, she cried loudly and continuously, she tore her robe and moved into her brother Absalom's home and lived in desolation. Tamar's grieving season was filled with wailing, despair, and hopelessness. She was ashamed and disgraced.

Scripture indicates all of this. Once she was put out of the Amnon's home, the Bible says she tore her robe. The significance of the torn robe was to illustrate the deep sense of separation she felt from what she had been before. Those elaborately decorative robes of virgins during that period indicated the virgins' high value and significance. As Tamar cried, she wept about how in her mind she had been ripped from her previous status.

The tearing also created uneven, jagged edges on the cloth itself. This torn cloth indicated a situation she felt could not be repaired. She wept over her lost status and framed the loss with the idea that this cannot be repaired. These symbolic realities create the frame for her hopeless posture what is not clearly spelled out is if she was willing to recover despite her horrible situation.

Ultimately, our recovery hinges on perspective. The more we can draw on the hope of recovery, during the grieving process, the more we prepare ourselves for recovery. Let me say this again, while you are facing the jagged, ripped, damaged places that have resulted, the key is to remain hopeful about what is ahead. Like TAMAR, if we cannot gather the smallest amount of hope WHILE WE ARE grieving, we run the risk of damaging our ability to recover. The scripture even goes on to say that Tamar lived in desolation.

It is so important to understand that the way we grieve, the process of grieving is indelibly connected to our resources and ability to recover. The scripture says that not only did Tamar not recover, but her ultimate outcome was also dramatically worse. Where she had previously had companionship and honor, she now lived in disgrace and desolation.

We must not overlook the impact of the grieving process and our responsibility to ourselves to grieve well. Yes, we have a responsibility, whenever it is in our power, to do what I call 'grieve well. This is not always possible. Abuse children may not be positioned to grieve well, families that experience several traumas at one time may not be positioned to grieve well, people that have not access to pastoral care or counseling may not be positioned to grieve well, but those of us that can, should.

This section was written to add this timeless truth to the prescription. Greif is an inherit part of loss and loss is an inherent part of life. In the best offensive positions, we will face the challenge of requiring our grief process to serve our ultimate recovery, by holding onto hopefulness for the future. By now, it should be clearer why this strategy is offensive. A good portion of the principles we discussed are decisions made BEFOREHAND, to be as prepared as possible for "the unexpected".

From my own life, I have suffered the fallout from grief that ran amok. My grief became discouragement, then depression, then despair and would have soon reached desolation. I realize HOLY SPIRIT'S guidance was a rescue mission from what could have become for me a life of desperation and desolation.

How do we make this practical? By seeking a place of rest in Abba God that can withstand the issues of life. Study the Word of God. Decide to increase relationship with the Father through worship. Ask God for directions on how and when to seek recovery. Understand and be confident, no life event alone has the power to render us desolate and unproductive. Refuse to be stuck! Kick, cry, scream, do whatever it takes to break that barrier, but declare the promises of God for your life and your future, early and often. Our access to His grace is unlimited. Access it. Use His strength to build an offensive strategy and REFUSE to be desolate.

Just like most liquid medications, the truth about our contribution to the recovery processes of our lives may be difficult to swallow but will benefit us in the end. The reality is, like Tamar, we probably know someone that had a life-devastating event and was not able to recover. That person might even be us. Millions of people are stuck, walking around corporate America with ripped robes, under their designer suits and dresses. Desolate does not suggest paralyzed or comatose, only unproductive in the purpose of God. This is not the place to settle. Let us make this commitment now: whenever loss crosses the path of my life, I will do everything in my power to grieve well.

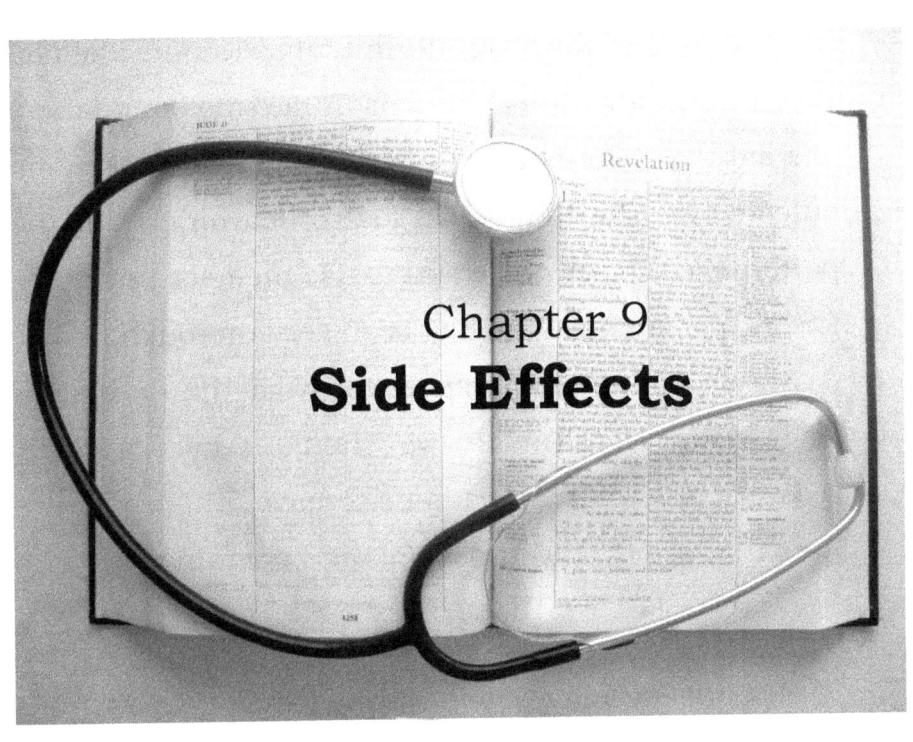

Chapter 9
Side Effects

How else can we proactively avoid the life of desolation that Tamar lived? How can we become comfortable in life knowing unexpected events happen all the time? If I still expect to avoid living in the ruins of the past, is this even possible? Most definitely!

This is why we are so grateful to Tamar. She has become our advocate to help us frame safe boundaries, she left many hints as to how we can avoid the same outcome as she did. Our goal of learning from the patterns left in scripture and to use them as guidelines for our personal safety, has been very thorough.

We should also expect to avoid the desolation that existed for Tamar; we should expect a **FULL** recovery process that leads us to have full, productive lives that are filled with vision and hopefulness.

> *1 Peter 1:7 – That the trial of your faith, being much more precious than of gold that perisheth, though it be tried with fire, might be found unto praise and honour and glory at the appearing of Jesus Christ:*

> *Romans 8:28 (VOICE) – We are confident that God is able to orchestrate everything*

to work toward something good and beautiful when we love Him and accept His invitation to live according to His plan.

Isaiah 43:2 (NLT) – When you go through deep waters, I will be with you. When you go through rivers of difficulty, you will not drown. When you walk through the fire of oppression, you will not be burned up; the flames will not consume you.

2 Thessalonians 3:3 (NLT) – But the Lord is faithful; he will strengthen you and guard you from the evil one.

Isaiah 53:4-5 – Surely He hath borne our griefs, and carried our sorrows: yet we did esteem Him stricken, smitten of God, and afflicted. But H was wounded for our transgressions, He was bruised for our iniquities: the chastisement of our peace was upon Him; and with His stripes we are healed.

> *Hebrews 4:15 – For we have not an High Priest which cannot be touched with the feeling of our infirmities; but was in all points tempted like as we are, yet without sin*

After that tragic event, after that unexpected occurrence, after being forced into an inappropriate relationship. After being disgraced and shamed and minimized and assaulted. After being violated, after being damaged and betrayed, YOU ARE STILL HERE! It is no small accomplishment that we have arrived on the other side of these things.

The Old Testament indicates another scripture that bolsters our understanding to this key to avoiding the place where we never recover:

> *Proverbs 23:7 – As a man thinketh in his heart so is he.*

What a powerfully profound statement of truth; it is one of the most liberating truths in Scripture. This scripture makes us fully aware not only of our ability and responsibilities for vision but also our power to create a life that aligns with the rich promises in the Word of God by how we think.

American culture can create intoxicating illusions of change beginning from the outside. For instance, some may think that starting a new business is as simple as having capital and a business plan. We will not suggest that these resources are not pivotal for an entrepreneur, however we do know if the mind of that entrepreneur does not begin to think along the lines of a successful business owner and maintain the infrastructure of the business, it would not be stable. This is why the scripture at its essence is so deeply powerful because it indicates that the genesis of any transformative moment has its origin in how we think.

Let's look at that more closely and restate it: The origin of any transformation in life has its origin in how we think. This scripture sits in opposition to most of the widely accepted ideas in modern culture. Societal norms dictate that we are to hinge our outcomes and our personal value, based on how we are perceived. The truth is, how we think of ourselves, how we think of our circumstance, even how we think of traumatic and brutal situations will determine our ability to transform personally, professionally and emotionally. Our outcome, whether we are desolate and unproductive or recover and flourish, is based on us as individuals and how we make our minds anew.

As Believers, we are given a full release to be free from all victimizing lifestyles and ways of operating, if we allow the Word and its unchanging truth to shape how we think. Knowing this is a useful exercise to consider in what could contribute to us having desolate outcomes. We see today what hints Tamar left in scripture regarding the process of her thinking that led to her later desolation. Even though this is a sharp reality, in the words of the Greek philosopher Epictetus:

It is not what happens to you, but how you react to it that matters!

This statement drives the point home, especially for the born-again Believer. The weight of any reaction to any event in life is directly related to how we choose to think... our actions and our whole way of existing originates in how we think. If we pair this truth with what we see in the account of Tamar, we can understand how we can benefit from looking closely at hints of how she thought about the situation in her life and how she subsequently ended up living in desolation.

The desolation, isolation, fear, and hopelessness we see describing Tamar after her attack is reflected in the words used to describe the reminder of her life.

How we think is the engine that ultimately drives recovery. The mindset that is victimized, by definition, embraces the harm done to it at the hand of another is not a mindset that is prepared to overcome and recover.

We have what it takes to overcome! The scripture says that we do not conquer, we are more than conquerors (Romans 8:37). How does this scripture contribute to this idea? The word conquer in scripture implies becoming the ruling power over something. This statement is written without condition, so it applies to circumstances in life from the least to the greatest. This scripture includes all ideas and all traumatic circumstances. This scripture has held its place of truth, without WAVERNG, for generations because it is truth. WE CAN DO MORE THAN CONQUER WHEN FACED WITH ADVERSITY.

How can the Bible assure us of this second "superpower" ability? Jesus Christ's ministry was, amongst other things, the way we received authority to thrive in the face of adversity. It is in this authority of the Believer that we must rely on when our circumstances seem more powerful than what our strength can handle. We must realize that when we are set as Kingdom citizens, we have access to the grace needed to recover and our ultimate goal is not to simply recover but to thrive.

Let us go back to Tamar's account for one last point. Are there hints that point to her way of thinking.? In verse 13 of 2 Samuel, it states:

> *As for me, how could I get rid of my shame and disgrace? And you, you will be considered one of the fools in Israel. So now, just speak to the king [about taking me as your* wife], for he will not withhold me from you."

The beginning of the verse says, "as for me," which is more clearly interpreted as "based on my part in this situation." Tamar's words in this scripture expose the first time we get a glimpse of how she may have been thinking in the aftermath.

If we call this her 'self-talk', we see Tamar questioning HER PART in this atrocity. How did she have a part? The way I read it, she was deceived and tricked, viciously attacked and disgraced. Add to that she was strategized against and amid this evil, she is recorded using words that suggested she had some responsibility.

The truth is anyone with this mindset is subject to this same error in thinking that both Tamar and I had. Oftentimes, if we have been abused, mistreated, rejected, or made to feel inadequate by evil, damaged people, systemic oppression, racially based biases, a victimized mindset lurking in the background of our lives will surely be activated. This WAY OF THINKING shows up when we have thought this way BEFORE a traumatic event, or it can attach itself as a result of the event; ultimately its ability to produce in our lives is totally up to us.

Wait! Hear me out. I know it may seem like I am saying – if you are victimized, then the ultimate outcome of being rendered helpless versus fully recovering is totally up to you. That is exactly what I am saying. What I am not saying is that the initial act of victimization is your responsibility. It is not yours to own or to be accountable for it. If, however, in the aftermath of that experience we embrace a victim mentality, that independent choice is ours.

Whenever we implode mentally with a sense of responsibility for someone else's decision, we are being victimized by our way of thinking. The shame was not hers to own; the shame was on Amnon and his wicked plan. The disgrace was not hers to be burdened by; it would be a disgraceful act carried out by anyone that shunned her because of what happened. They would be acting disgracefully.

We do have a part to play. We have a responsibility to use the principles in this prescription. We have the responsibility to create new boundaries. We have the responsibility to mature with clarity and gain wisdom. However, if we choose to focus on distortions of blame, we will continue to be victims in our minds.

Let us not be mistaken. Victim mindsets do considerable emotional damage if left unchecked. They render us hopeless and perpetually helpless by assigning the burden of someone else's evil decision to our life.

Look how soon after this mindset was exposed did the scripture describe how Tamar lived. Our mindsets are intricately connected to what we produce in life. Victim mentality will hide behind the masquerade of self-proclaimed 'strong people', but if you allow them to speak, how they actually think will always speak out, just like it did with Tamar.

Can I say with certainty, no one will ever deal with us based on bias, or assault us, or harm us relationally? No I cannot, but I can say if we practice offensive strategies and guard against a victim mentality, we are in the best position to recover.

If you have never had a victimized mentality like I did, then this section may not resonate with you. But for those of us who have been traumatized by others' decisions and then by our own thoughts, this truth is a huge area of awakening. I can put exclamations around this next sentence because it is resounding and forever true.

Guard yourself from the victimized mindset and people that have them.

I cannot express how often Holy Spirit would guide me and teach me by exposing my self-talk. It was the dominant voice that led to years of personal emotional enslavement and obligation. It was a whole mess!

At the time, I did not have the capacity to look in the face of the incident and be hopeful. I did not have the where-with-all to take all the medicine. I did not have the clarity of thought to reject self-sabotaging thoughts and properly release the responsibility to the person that was accountable. I did not have the courage to stand up for myself and confront my "Amnon." I needed every single ounce of this prescription and Holy Spirit walked me through to my liberty.

Freedom is our inheritance.
Victory is our final answer.

When Holy Spirit prescribed me this scripture and this understanding, I was finally clear how I should move forward. I will be honest and say I had not expected such hard work. The confrontations of my old thoughts and confrontation of my "Amnon", holding myself accountable to protect myself in the ways I have access to was a real effort in the strength of Holy Spirit. Despite the uncertain days, despite the fear of adding the wisdom of this experience to my life, I have not looked back. I honestly have not. I enjoy the liberty of this wholeness in ways that bring me blissful joy.

Now for the last doses:

- Disallow any thought or reflection that mimics the 'as for me' mentality.
- Reassure your heart that you will and can recover.
- Make sure to do your forgiveness work.
- Refuse to speak from injured emotions, declare the promises of God, relentlessly.
- Dismiss the notion that we can "delete" the entirety of an unexpected event. As we do our work in these areas, to delete or get rid of the experience would also get rid of the wisdom we've gained.
- Refuse desolation.

Now, let us wash it down:

- Ultimately recovery is a choice not based in the level of the violation but in the yielding to the power of forgiveness and seeking wisdom.

- We are designed by God as powerful resilient people; offensive strategies in life help us protect that power.
- Bitterness and hatred are not real emotional payoffs; they are forfeitures of substantive healing.
- Self-reliance is not a substitute when we need the power and guidance of HOLY SPIRIT.
- Wisdom is hinged on the heels of clarity. As you heal, continue to wipe away thoughts that seek to cloud your perspective.

If any part of the situation was fueled by naivete or personal bad judgement, forgive yourself as well. You are most worthy of full love and forgiveness.

Prayer of Salvation

It would be my pleasure and honor to introduce you to the God that has saved and transformed my life! Did you know that Jesus Christ died on the Cross so that you and I might have eternal life? The Bible declares that if we confess with our mouth and believe in our heart that Jesus Christ is Lord, then we would be saved. It is a promise and covenant between God and His people.

"...If you confess with your mouth, "Jesus is Lord," and believe in your heart that God raised him from the dead, you will be saved. (Romans 10:9 – 11, NIV).

If you are ready to receive Jesus as your Savior, say this prayer:

Heavenly Father, I come to You in the Name of Your Son Jesus Christ. You said in Your Word that whosoever shall call upon the name of the Lord shall be saved. (Romans 10:13) Father, I am calling on Jesus right now. I believe He died on the cross for my sins, that He was raised from the dead on the third day, and He's alive right now. Lord Jesus, I am asking You now, come into my heart. Live Your life in me and through me. I repent of my sins and surrender myself totally and completely to You. Heavenly Father, by faith I now confess Jesus Christ as my new Lord and from this day forward, I dedicate my life to serving Him.

Biography

Dr. Cyrene Wright is excited to share her passion for international outreach, medical mission, and healing (physically and spiritually) with the nations of the world. Her passion for domestic and international service is sincere and sacrificial, a true reflection of the nature of Christ.

She was chosen by Harpo Studios Production, Inc. to travel with Oprah Winfrey to the Addis Ababa Fistula Hospital in Addis Ababa, Ethiopia, the Horn of Africa. This experience allowed her to see first-hand the travesty of unrepaired obstetric complications. Dr. Wright was later invited to appear on the Oprah Winfrey Show to share this awesome life-changing experience.

She continues her drive to activate and galvanize everyone into their local and global purpose. Dr. Wright, a tremendous visionary is also a leading voice in promoting health maintenance and disease prevention and can be found sharing these ideas on social media platforms.

While in the United States, Dr. Wright is committed to bringing excellent health care information and service to the medically underserved and encourages community-centered health education through free clinic programs

Dr. Wright is a graduate of the Chicago Medical School/RFUHS, Waukegan IL and the current President/CEO of Mission5511, Inc. and THE G.L.A.D Academy.

www.ingramcontent.com/pod-product-compliance
Lightning Source LLC
Chambersburg PA
CBHW050436010526
44118CB00013B/1558